WRITE YOUR OWN...

MYSTERY

PIE CORBETT

ILLUSTRATED BY
PETER BAILEY

Chrysalis Chil

To Teddy, who likes a good mystery.

First published in Great Britian in 2004 by Chrysalis Children's Books,
An imprint of Chrysalis Books Group,
The Chrysalis Building, Bramley Rd, London W10 6SP

Editorial manager: Joyce Bentley
Series editor: Debbie Foy
Editor: Joe Fullman
Designer: Sophie Wilkins
Illustrator: Peter Bailey

ISBN 1 84458 325 2

British Library Cataloguing in Publication Data for
this book is available from the British Library.

Printed and bound in China

10 9 8 7 6 5 4 3 2 1

CONTENTS

PUZZLING PLOTS
THINKING ABOUT MYSTERY

Outside it was dark, the moon covered by filmy clouds. Amy shivered as she walked down towards the bottom of the lane. She was just passing the old church hall when she noticed a light, flickering in the window. She tugged Sam away from a tree that he had been sniffing.

Amy knew that the church hall was never used on a Tuesday evening. She had walked past the hall every Tuesday for at least four years and there had never been anybody there before. She crouched down and pulled Sam close to her. She could just see the light – it was a lantern and someone was waving it back and forth as if they were signalling something. Suddenly, the lantern went out and she heard the distinct sound of breaking glass...

What is going on in the old church hall? Is someone in danger? Does this sort of story make you want to keep reading? Do you enjoy watching films full of clues and suspense that are only solved at the end? If you like puzzling plots and cliffhangers, how about trying to write one yourself? This book will help you write a really gripping mystery.

WHAT IS A MYSTERY?

Mystery stories are packed with scares, suspense and fast-paced action that keep you right on the edge of your seat. A mystery story may be:

☆ a detective mystery
  or 'whodunnit'
  In these stories a private
  eye or detective is usually
  working against time to solve
  an impossible robbery or
  curious crime!

☆ an adventure mystery
  In these, a great adventure is wrapped
  around a mystery. Perhaps
  the main characters see a
  strange light in a vacant
  house and they set about
  solving the mystery with
  many thrills and spills on
  the way!

WHAT DO I NEED TO WRITE MY OWN MYSTERY?

The great thing about being a writer is that you don't need much equipment, just a writing journal or notebook, a pen and a place to write. However, the most important thing that you need is the ability to daydream and think up great stories! Mystery writers are also like good detectives – always on the look out for characters, settings, details and ideas.

CURIOUSER AND CURIOUSER...

Like all stories, a mystery has certain key ingredients:

1. The problem

In a mystery story the problem usually occurs early on. The mystery 'problem' could be:

☆ a kidnap;
☆ a robbery;
☆ a weird happening;
☆ an unearthed secret.

2. The investigation

Once the mystery problem has occurred, the rest of the story is an investigation into what has happened. It is the main character who tries to solve the mystery.

3. Clues and red herrings

A mystery writer lays plenty of clues that lead to the mystery being solved. Some of the clues will be genuine and some will need to be 'red herrings'. These are clues that are intended to mislead the reader!

4. Flashbacks

These are used in mystery stories to explain what has happened in the past. Flashbacks allow the characters to go back in time and explain to the reader how the mysterious events unfolded...

5. Suspense

Mystery writers pack their stories with suspense. The reader is constantly wondering what will happen and how the mystery will be solved.

6. Cliffhangers

Cliffhangers are there to keep you reading! They usually come at the end of a section or chapter and leave the main characters at such an exciting or dangerous moment that the reader is desperate to find out what happens next!

7. Mystery characters

Most mystery stories have the following key characters to make the mystery work:

☆ the 'sleuth' or detective

A mystery story has a main character who tries to solve the mystery. It could be a real detective or an ordinary person who acts like a detective.

☆ the villain

This is the person responsible for the mystery. The villain could be an evil person or it could be something more innocent like a magpie that steals jewels!

☆ the suspects

The suspects are characters who might have been responsible for the mystery. It is good for your story if the suspects appear to have a reason for committing the crime. This is called a motive.

CUNNING READS

If you want to write mystery stories then you will need to read plenty. The more you read, the more you will become familiar with the basic ingredients that a mystery writer needs. Try to read as many mystery stories as possible from this list before planning your own story:

☆ *The Rat-a-tat Mystery*, Enid Blyton
☆ *Sam, The Girl Detective: The Case of the Missing Mummy*, Tony Bradman
☆ *Bug Muldoon Stories*, Paul Shipton
☆ *Diamond Brothers Stories*, Anthony Horowitz
☆ *Holes*, Louis Sachar
☆ *Harry Potter Series*, J K Rowling
☆ *The Castafiore Emerald*, Herge
☆ *Mystery Stories*, edited by Helen Cresswell

KEEP A WRITING JOURNAL

Writers are always on the lookout for ideas. Most writers keep a writing journal. This is a place for jotting down ideas before they get forgotten.

Look out for:

☆ unusual characters who might make great villains or suspects;
☆ strange places where weird things might happen;
☆ curious things that people say or do;
☆ news stories about local crimes or happenings that you could use as a basis for your mystery 'problem'.

WRITING TIP

Get a cardboard box and use it to store possible 'clues'. These could be any odd or unusual items you find. When you come to write you may not use all the items in your box, but they might give you some ideas. You might save:

★ a black feather;
★ a scrap of a letter;
★ a match box;
★ a strand of hair from a barbed wire fence;
★ a strange photograph;
★ a button found on the pavement;
★ a news clipping about a burglary.

PLOT TRIGGERS

Always be on the hunt for ideas that will trigger your story into action. One way to do this is to read newspapers or watch the news on television and make a note of any unusual stories. Another way is to daydream up some lists of ideas, for example:

Supposing...

☆ you hear an odd noise coming from an empty house;
☆ coming home from school you see two men carrying a rolled up carpet out of a deserted house;
☆ you get a letter warning you not to make friends with the new girl at school;
☆ the new teacher is overheard talking about kidnapping;
☆ a conjuror performs a disappearing trick and does not reappear.

1. Start your writing journal with a list of your favourite mystery books. Make notes on how the author:

★ creates suspense and uses cliffhangers;
★ keeps up a fast pace;
★ drops in clues;
★ uses 'red herrings' to mislead you from the real villain;
★ ties up the loose threads at the end.

2. Now start collecting some possible triggers to fire up the plot. Cut out extracts from newspapers that could provide plots and stick them into your journal.

3. Make a list of 'supposing...' ideas in your writing journal.

TRUE OR FALSE?

★ **A RED HERRING IS A SMALL, RED FISH.**

★ **A CLIFFHANGER IS A BAD MOUNTAIN CLIMBER.**

WRITERS AT WORK

CREATING YOUR OWN MYSTERY

All writers have five 'servants' to help them when they sit down to write a mystery: who? where? when? what? and how?

1. Who?
Think about your characters, especially the sleuth, the villain and the other suspects. Draw up a 'gallery' for your main characters so that they become 'real' people to you! Be on the lookout for the sort of thing that makes people look suspicious and make a note of these details.

For example:
☆ a hat pulled down to hide a person's face;
  ☆ a coat that almost hides the person wearing it;
☆ a person who is always looking over their shoulder;
☆ someone who ducks behind a wall....

2. Where?

Next, think about where to set the story. The setting for the mystery 'problem' should suggest mystery and secrecy, for example: a dark alley, an empty house, a lonely harbour, a damp cave or a deserted clifftop.

Often the main mystery involves a specific part of the setting such as a hidden door, escape tunnel or secret lever, that is vital to creating the mystery. For this reason, many writers draw maps of the mystery setting so that when they write, they can describe the place in detail.

WRITING TIP

Think carefully about the main setting for the mystery problem. Try to persuade your family to actually visit a place that could act as your mystery setting. Take your journal and draw a sketch or map, making notes of specific details.

3. When?

Most stories are written in the past tense. This makes it sound as if the story has already happened. For example: *Layla watched the deserted house every night and waited for the green van to return.*

At the end of the story you may use a 'flashback' in which the sleuth takes the reader right back in time to explain what happened.

4. What?

You need some ideas about the central mystery in your story. This is called the plot outline, such as: A robbery takes place at the local jewellery store but no windows were broken, no alarms went off, and even the safe remained closed...

WRITING TIP

Make a list of great mysteries that have really happened. For example, in the Bermuda Triangle mystery, a number of planes and ships disappeared and were never found again! Finding out about real mysteries may spark your imagination.

5. How?

Once you have decided on the mystery 'problem' you will need to be clear about who did it, why they did it and how it happened?

Think up some clever clues that you will reveal to suggest 'whodunnit' or what has happened. Of course, you will need to plant a few 'red herrings' to make your reader think someone else is the villain, before you reveal the villain's true identity at the end!

Let's think a bit more about some of these five 'servants'.

CREATING MYSTERY CHARACTERS

Your characters are one of the most important parts of the story. In mystery stories there are three main character types that you need to think about. You can have more than one sleuth, villain or suspect, of course, but try not to have too many or it will be difficult to make them all sound real.

Before writing, think about:

1. The character's names

The names you choose can often suggest something about the character. For instance, Dr Hate sounds like somebody not to be tangled with! You could also use the name to hide the character's real intentions and to fool the reader. So old Mrs Perkins might not be such a nice old lady – she could be the villain of the piece!

Your sleuth character might have a very ordinary name like Tom Stannard or Jo Hanway and your villain may have an unusual name like Bodger O'Neill, Smudge Baxter or Fingers McClary. But there are no hard-and-fast rules, so spend some time thinking up names and think about how that character might look and act!

2. Character type

Now decide what kind of person each character is. In your 'gallery' you could label each character as a certain type: shy, lonely, aggressive, happy-go-lucky, brainy, spiteful, mean, a misery guts etc. It can be fun to select contrasting characters, so if one is bossy then make the other one timid!

THE SUPERSLEUTH

The sleuth or 'detective' is the main character who will probably witness the mystery problem and then set off in search of the answer. As your main character, your sleuth will need to be someone likeable so that your readers stay interested in him or her.

A sleuth character needs to have a good reason for wanting to solve the mystery and it is likely that they are good at solving mysteries. They should also have the following supersleuth qualities:

☆ good at working out clues

You will need to show your sleuth's thinking as they tussle with the mystery problem. For example: *According to Mrs Jenkins, Bill had been at the library first thing in the morning – but Jake now knew that this had to be impossible....*

☆ asks lots of questions

Your sleuth should not be afraid of asking questions to help solve the mystery. For example: *So where did Sam go? Had he been kidnapped? So far, we had drawn a blank but I felt the only way to proceed was to keep asking around the village...*

☆ extremely observant

Sleuths need to give good descriptions of suspects, places and events. For example: *There was something familiar about the way his eyes narrowed like a hawk. Then I saw a flash of gold – his teeth clicked together and his tongue flickered like a snake...*

WRITING TIP

Here are some useful phrases to show that your sleuth is on the case:

He noticed that···

It soon became obvious to me that···

He stared at···

I noticed that···

It was clear to Tom that···

There was something familiar about the way···

THE SUSPICIOUS SUSPECTS

To lead the reader off the scent, it is a good idea to have a handful of suspects who your readers can believe might have been responsible for the mystery. Before writing, it may be useful to start drawing up a 'gallery' of suspects and make notes under each one, about their appearance, who they are, what they do, how old they are and so on. You will need to think of reasons why each suspect might have been involved in the 'crime'. These reasons will need to be dropped into the story as you go along so that the readers begin to suspect.... the wrong person! For instance, if you had a mystery in which a painting is stolen from a gallery, you might have a suspicious art dealer who happened to be in the vicinity at the time.

THE VILLAINOUS VILLAIN

This person takes their place among your gallery of suspects and will need a good reason for committing the crime. Try not to make the real villain appear obviously evil; it can be more effective to make the villain someone

who you would never suspect! This keeps the reader
guessing and adds a surprising twist at the end. Your
villainous villain could be:

☆ a kind, old lady;

☆ a quiet and studious librarian;

☆ a mischievous child;

☆ a respected person such as a vicar or headteacher;

☆ your best friend's mum.

WRITING TIP

Having too many characters can be a
disadvantage as it may be difficult for your
reader to distinguish between them. Try to stick to one or
two sleuths and the same number of villains, this way you
can concentrate on making them 'goodies' or 'baddies'.

MONSTROUS MOTIVES

To make the mystery seem 'real' you will need to think
about the motives of your characters. A motive is what
makes a person do something. All your characters should
have motives. For example:

☆ the sleuth

   What is the sleuth's motive for solving the crime? Are
   they just curious or does the mystery problem affect
   them in some way?

☆ the villain

   Why did the villain steal the money? Are they jealous,
   greedy, a compulsive robber, or perhaps they need the
   money for a specific reason?

☆ the suspects

To make the mystery harder to solve, it is helpful if the suspects also have motives. This can lead the reader in the wrong direction!

STUNNING SPECIAL EFFECTS

All mystery writers have a few techniques which can create different effects in their writing. Try using these special effects to make your mystery more powerful.

1. Similes

A simile is a descriptive way of comparing one thing to another. Either use the word 'like': *His teeth looked like old gravestones.* Or use the word 'as': *His teeth were as crooked as old gravestones.*

2. Metaphors

A metaphor is a bit like a simile. The difference is that, in a simile, you say that one thing is like another but, in a metaphor, you say one thing *is* another. For example, this is a simile: *His teeth were as crooked as old gravestones.* This is a metaphor: *His crooked, gravestone teeth shone in the moonlight.* Both similes and metaphors help to create powerful pictures in your readers' minds.

3. Personification

Personification makes an object seem human. You either describe an object as if it looks human, for example: *The huge cave mouth gaped at him.* Or describe it as if it is

doing something that a human might do. For example:
The oak's branches pointed, as if to scold us.

4. Alliteration

Alliteration is the repetition of similar sounds. This can be useful in creating atmosphere in your story. In this example, the 'sh' sound is repeated:
The shadows shivered and shook their heads.

HOOK YOUR READER!

Have you ever started a book and given up after a few pages because it didn't capture your interest? You need to 'hook' your reader with an exciting event early on!

Writers use 'hooks' to grab the reader's attention. They are sentences that drop a hint that something is going to happen. A hook tantalises the reader into wanting to read on to see what will happen. Here are some examples that might make a reader think who? why? what?

☆ *Coombe Drive was built on an old burial ground. It was supposed to be*

haunted. But Jake had always laughed at such stories;

☆ *No one ever walked on Grazeney Marsh. It was said to have claimed many lives...*

☆ *They could hear the dog barking late at night. But no one had ever seen it...*

TIME TO WRITE

1 1. In your writing journal:

★ Create a character 'gallery' for your main characters – sleuth, suspects and villain, including a name and some special details about them and what type of person they are. Beside the characters make a list of possible motives for their crimes!

★ Write down some ideas for settings for the different scenes in your story.

★ Jot down some basic plot outlines to choose from.

2 Dream up some ideas for thrilling 'hooks' that will capture your readers and keep them on the edge of their seats!

TRICKS OF THE TRADE
HOW TO MYSTIFY YOUR READERS!

All the best writers do a lot of thinking before they put pen to paper. This chapter reveals a few tricks of the trade that writers of mysteries use to mystify their readers by creating realistic characters and exciting settings.

MAKING YOUR CHARACTERS 'REAL'

1. Describing your characters

To make your characters seem real, you need to describe their appearance. The details you mention should suggest something about the type of person they are. For example, a shady character might wear dark clothing, or a 'showy' person might wear loud, bright colours.

☆ what their features are like

Describe your characters' features. For example:

Eyes: dark, brooding, grey, sharp, mean, cruel...

Mouth: thin lips, tense, like a slit, tight, broad grin...

Teeth: white, jagged, one gold tooth, uneven...

Hair: slicked back, greasy, thin, glossy, cropped...

Hands: like a bird's claw, thin, gnarled, bony, fat and stubby, grimy, chewed fingernails...

☆ **how they walk**
How your characters walk can suggest what kind of character they are. For example, *Bitzer Malone sidled over to the gate...* or *Tim Poplar strode into the room.*

☆ **how they talk**
Your characters' voices could be high-pitched, squeaky, whispering or slow; booming, grating, rasping or sing-song.

WRITING TIP

Try using a 'sentence of three' to describe your characters. For example:

Mrs Maples was wearing a shiny overcoat, black wellingtons and a peaked hat. **Or,** Buster McVey had slicked back hair, brooding eyes and hands like shovels.

☆ **use special details**
Small details are important when building up a picture of a character. For example:
His small, diamond ring sparkled in the lights...
Her shiny, snakeskin shoes squeaked with every step...
The ends of his spectacles had been chewed almost to nothing...
A red, silk hanky poked out of his top pocket...

2. How your characters act

Think carefully about how different characters will behave. Shy people may want to withdraw but bossy and aggressive characters will act quite differently. You can build your character's personality by showing how they act. See how these two pieces of writing can convey, for example, either a confident or a shy person:

Jake snatched up his coat, dashed out of the door and rushed to his car. 'I might have guessed this would happen,' he snapped, 'I don't trust Baxter Bloggs an inch!'

Si picked up his coat, quietly opened the door and made his way to the car. 'Oh dear, this is a mess,' he wailed, 'I hope Baxter Bloggs isn't involved in this...'

WRITING TIP

Use an 'ing' clause to add on to a simple sentence to describe what someone is doing or thinking. This is called a 'supporting action'. For example:

Tom ate his breakfast, wondering where he should start searching.

Mr Potts began to study the map, noticing that there was a forest in Bigham.

3. Making your characters talk

Each character should have a distinctive voice so that the reader can easily identify who is speaking. You can do this in several ways. For example:

☆ Try finding a few unusual phrases that a character might use, e.g. *'Oh rats,' snapped Dr Hatelove.*

☆ Use powerful speech verbs to show how something is said, e.g. *'Put it down,' barked the policeman.*

☆ Use adverbs to add extra information to the words that mean 'said', for example: *'I admit I was wrong' he replied reluctantly.*

Put it down!

4. Use gossip!

You can also build a character by having other people – possibly two minor characters – gossiping. For instance, in this sentence, another character gossips about Tim providing more information for the reader:

'Poor Tim, he's been so miserable since his dog was kidnapped last Christmas...'

5. Use a 'backstory' technique

This is useful for dropping clues into the story about a character's past life. They provide a hint or clue about the background to your characters. You could mention:

☆ an object

For example: *Miss Plum picked up her karate trophy and placed it back on the mantlepiece.*

☆ an old photo

For example: *Barney glanced back at the photo. In it, he could see Mrs Grainger, about to board Concorde.*

☆ a memory

For example: *'Last time I was here, it was raining,' said Mr Gargery as he took off his jacket.*

☆ an item of clothing

For example: *Sandy adjusted his yachting cap...*

6. Describe your characters' thoughts and feelings

Another way to build up a character is to show what they are thinking. Here are some useful openers:

Tom thought back to when...
Major Morse wondered whether...
Smudge reckoned that...
Mrs Bottomley recalled that...
Tim felt there was something that just did not add up...
Madeleine puzzled over the idea...

Your sleuth character will be thinking about the mystery and trying to piece the clues together. If you reveal their thinking then the reader can

become a 'supersleuth' and join in with the detective work!
For example:

Trudy knew that the church hall should have been empty that night but it was also clear now that the florists had been delivering flowers for the wedding that was taking place there the following day. She also knew that earlier the same afternoon there had been a robbery at old Mrs Jenkins house. Was there a connection? She didn't know but she knew how she might find out...

Did you notice the question: *'Was there a connection?'* Sleuths should always be asking questions! Asking questions will set your readers wondering and lead the action forwards.

WRITING TIP
Make a police file report for your suspects. It could look like this:

POLICE FILE REPORT

Name of suspect:	Dr Hatelove
Age:	50
Address:	The Mall Practice, 12 Harley Street, London, EC11
Description:	Small, bald, piercing green eyes
Special identifying marks:	Scar on left cheek
Alibi:	Was operating in his clinic
Motive:	Greed

UNCANNY SETTINGS

You will need to create some mysterious settings for your story. What sort of places do you know that might be suitable? You could choose somewhere that is lonely or you could have the mystery happen in an everyday place like a school canteen! Near where I live there is:

☆ a disused bus shelter;

☆ an old mine pit;

☆ a quarry;

☆ an old abattoir.

Once you have decided what settings to use in your story, it's a good idea to sketch a simple map of the area, showing the places where your characters live and where the story takes place.

BRINGING SETTINGS ALIVE

Setting is very important in mystery stories as it can really add to the atmosphere! Here are some tips:

1. Use mysterious-sounding place names

A good idea is to look for real place names on a map, for example: *Darkfell Hall, Goldenacres or Monkswood Path.*

2. Use familiar settings

If you base your mystery setting on a place you already know then it will be easier to give details about it. For example, perhaps you have visited a castle, a clifftop, an old school or factory that you could use as a setting!

3. Describe what you see and hear

Try to mention some details that are unusual or out of place. For example:

The curtains were all drawn shut. It looked as if the house was asleep. Paula could hear a low humming sound. It seemed to be coming from beneath the house! There was also a faint light coming from the bottom of the cellar door at the side of the house. She noticed a scrap of paper sticking out of the letterbox and went to investigate...

4. Use the weather

Weather helps build up atmosphere and a sense of mystery. For example:

The wild wind whipped the frost-glittered leaves across the lawn of the old mansion. The snowman that the children built yesterday looked lost and forlorn and the sky looked heavy and grey, as though it were in sympathy.

5. Use the time of day
Setting your mystery at certain times of the day helps create atmosphere.

The clouds wrapped themselves around the moon and Jake could only just make out the pavement ahead. He pulled his coat closer. The mist crept up from the river and the night-time noises had started again! Oh, where was Judy when he needed her...?

THE PLOT THICKENS...

Mystery writers use a number of special techniques to build up suspense, keeping the readers on the edge of their seats – baffled and curious until the very end!

1. Planting clues
You will need to 'plant' clues in the story – nothing too obvious or your reader will solve the mystery too easily. For example, you could use:

☆ a photograph, for example: *In the photo, he was wearing some sort of uniform...*

☆ a news clipping, for example: *Mrs Verity, a devoted church-goer and mother-of-three, was found guilty of robbery last week and jailed for five years…*

☆ a letter, for example: *'…but the strangest part was, I never, ever saw her again…'*

☆ gossip, for example: *'He used to be a teacher,' muttered Jake…*

2. Dropping red herrings!

A red herring is a misleading clue that might take the sleuth, and the reader, off in the wrong

direction. Mystery writers often use red herrings in mystery stories to mislead the reader and to keep everyone guessing.

3. Awesome alibis

All of your characters will need an alibi to prove that they could not possibly have been involved in the mystery! An alibi provides evidence that a person accused of a crime was somewhere else when it was committed.

Your sleuth character needs to discover where everyone was and what they were doing. Were they with someone else who could back up their story? Good alibis are ones where other people are involved.

Examples of good alibis might be:

☆ being at a party;

☆ being seen on a train or plane;

☆ talking on the phone to someone;

☆ shopping and being seen on CCTV cameras;

Your villain will need an alibi – but it will be false. For instance, the villain might claim to have been at work with the door closed and the radio on. In the end, it turns out that the villain climbed out of the window to carry out the deed...!

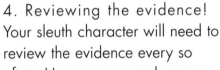

Decide what the villain's alibi will be and then work out what really happened.

4. Reviewing the evidence!
Your sleuth character will need to review the evidence every so often. Here are some phrases you might find useful:

I had little to go on, but I had a hunch about the old man...
We were no nearer discovering why...
Part of me still wondered whether...
According to her nothing had happened, but why did I still feel uneasy...?
Mrs Jenkins had told us nothing new, and yet...

5. Detective work
Use a detective's line in questioning to help channel the reader's thinking. For example:
Had he been asleep? Where had the sound of snoring been coming from? Was it true that the parrot could speak? Did Polly really hold the key to cracking the mystery wide open?

6. Cliffhangers

Cliffhangers are a key part of mysteries. They are exciting parts of a story where something dramatic occurs, leaving the reader desperate to read on and find out what happens. Usually cliffhangers occur at the end of a section or chapter. To write a cliffhanger you need to build up to a sudden turn of events right at the end of a paragraph. For example:

Kirsty walked over the road. She was still not sure why Dr Vix had wanted her to go back for the suitcase. It was raining hard now. She had her head down and so she did not see the van pull up or the two men leap out. The next thing she knew, she was grabbed from behind and a sack placed over her head. She too, had been kidnapped!

Did you notice how Kirsty was not looking where she was going as her mind was elsewhere? A useful technique when writing cliffhangers is to lead your character's attention somewhere else before the dramatic incident takes place. Some ideas for cliffhangers are:

☆ someone goes missing;
☆ something important is stolen;
☆ someone is grabbed or attacked;
☆ the car's brakes fail;
☆ the stairs collapse;
☆ someone yells in surprise.

7. Flashbacks

Flashbacks can be a good way of explaining events or filling in background detail. Often a character thinks back to a previous event. For example:

Tim thought back to the previous day when he had...
It had only been an hour ago that they had...
Wasn't it only a week since they had...
As far as she could recall...
She distinctly remembered that day because...

WRITING TIP

Don't worry if your story isn't long enough to be split up into chapters, you can still use cliffhangers to grip your readers. Write your main character into a possibly disastrous situation at the end of a paragraph, so that your readers have to read on to the next paragraph to find out what happens.

TIME TO WRITE

You are almost ready to start writing. Before you start, however, you need to map out your mystery story. Make notes in your writing journal under the following headings:

★ the mystery problem

What is the crime or mystery that needs solving? Is it a robbery, a kidnapping, a disappearance or some other kind of weird happening?

★ the main characters

Add more information to your gallery of characters. Think about how they talk, walk, act and any special details about their appearance. Do this for:

☆ the sleuth   ☆ the suspects   ☆ the villain

★ the setting

Decide on the setting for your mystery and think about how you can bring the setting 'alive'. Think about the weather and time of day too.

★ the motive

Be clear about what your characters' motives are. Why did the villain commit the crime? Why does the sleuth want to solve the mystery? Make sure some of your suspects have a motive too, so that your reader doesn't solve the mystery before the end of your story!

★ clues and red herrings

Make two columns in your journal. One should have a heading 'clues' and the other, 'red herrings'. Plan out your story listing the clues and red herrings that your sleuth will have to contend with, in order to solve the mystery!

PUTTING PEN TO PAPER

MAP OUT YOUR MYSTERY

Ready to start writing? Before you finally start, read this chapter. Each section will help you through a different stage in your mystery. It can help to think about your story in three sections:

The beginning where you introduce the characters and set up the mystery;
The middle in which the sleuth investigates and unearths clues;
The end where the clues pile up and the villain is revealed!

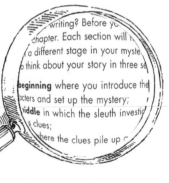

THE BAFFLING BEGINNING

Imagine if a mystery story opened like this: *Billy whistled a jolly tune as he walked to school. The birds were singing and Billy wondered what he was having for his supper that night...*

Doesn't exactly grip you, does it? The start of your story must really captivate your reader and make them itch to find out more! Here are some ideas:

1. Introduce your main character

Use the opening paragraph to introduce your main character, perhaps your sleuth? Try to build a picture of the character in the reader's mind. Think about how the character is feeling and show this through what they say and do. For example:

Brian looked down at his feet and saw they were red raw. From inside the flat, he could hear Mrs Swabey shuffling and scraping as she made her way down the corridor. At any moment the door would open and he would have to explain himself. Reluctantly, he waited.

2. Set the scene

The setting can create a tense atmosphere. Use specific details and don't forget to show the time of day and the weather as a backdrop. For example:

It was cold on deck but Valerie stood there for as long as she could. She watched the distant lights of the town, strung out along the coast like a thin necklace, disappear into the night. The ferry rolled slowly from side to side in a gentle rocking motion as it carved its way through the dark waters.

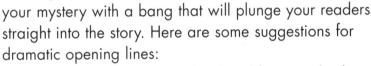

She waited on deck long after she saw her parents blur into the lights, blinking back her tears...

3. Use a dramatic event

You might want to start your mystery with a bang that will plunge your readers straight into the story. Here are some suggestions for dramatic opening lines:

☆ *As Gina sat down to eat her breakfast somebody screamed...*

☆ *Funnily enough, Brian was just getting into the bath when the river banks broke...*

☆ *The bank's alarm rang as a gang of four robbers burst into the vaults...*

☆ *A hand grabbed Val's ankle and held on so tightly that she yelled...*

4. Use dialogue

This can be a handy way to start a story off – especially if what is said helps to get the action going. For example:

'Help me, please' wailed Mrs Jones, 'someone has just made off with my garden gnome'.

'Don't worry, Mrs Jones,' I said reassuringly, 'We can always get you a replacement.'

'But you don't understand,' the old lady cried, 'that's where I keep my sapphire bracelet. But no-one knows that, except me...'

THE DASTARDLY DEED

Early on in the story you will need to introduce the mystery event or crime itself. Build up what happens gradually. It can help if your main character is doing something quite ordinary and then sees or hears something unusual which leads them to investigate. For example:

It was a cold Saturday afternoon and Michaela was raking up the leaves in the Baxters' garden. It was very hard work because the wind kept blowing them about.

Once the sack was full she dragged it to the end of the garden and tipped the leaves out onto the smouldering bonfire. They

fell like so many fragments of paper, in a tumble of reds and golds. As she was staring at the flames, she heard somebody moan. Her instinct was to duck down and freeze, but through the hedge she could just make out two men carrying something long and heavy between them and they were heading for a parked van....

WRITING TIP
Use a good story starter to get the action moving. In the first few paragraphs introduce the mystery. Right from the beginning you need to build your readers' curiosity so that they will want to read on.

THE MEDDLESOME MIDDLE

In a mystery story the middle part is usually about the sleuth trying to solve the crime or mystery. Think about this part of your story as a series of scenes. Each scene can become a chapter or section of the story. As your 'sleuth' character tries to solve the mystery, he or she may:

☆ travel to different places;
☆ interview suspects;
☆ search for clues;
☆ investigate the scene of the mystery;
☆ go undercover – the better to observe people!

To keep the reader in suspense, you will need to use cliffhangers so make sure you drop in exciting events as the story unfolds. Try ending a chapter or section on a cliffhanger. Each section or chapter will have the following shape:

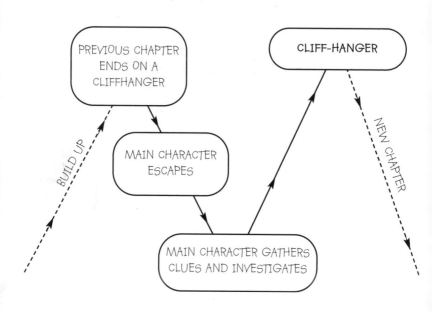

Your whole story will have this sort of shape:

While you are writing, you may find that sometimes your writing just flows, while on other occasions you get stuck. Don't worry, this happens to every writer. If you get stuck, you could try:

★ looking at your plan to see what is meant to happen next;

★ daydreaming the next section or making a new list of ideas for possible scenes;

★ writing the final line of your story and working back from there;

★ introducing a new setting;

★ making something unexpected happen.

WRITING SUSPENSE SCENES

Suspense scenes will be vital to building up the excitement in your mystery. Your main character will be looking for clues and this will take them into scary situations. For example:

Jake grabbed the rope belonging to the twins' treehouse den. Gripping tightly, he hauled himself up the old oak, crept carefully along a large branch and stopped

opposite the window. Pausing, he balanced himself and then leapt. But he missed! Grasping the window ledge, Jake clung on. It took all his effort to pull himself up, but in the end he managed to scramble through the open window and into the room.

It was pitch dark. It was too quiet. He stood still, listening to the thudding of his heart. At that moment, he heard a scratching sound that seemed to be coming from downstairs. Jake froze. Was it one of the Doberman Pinschers? Silently, he tiptoed on to the landing.

There was a light from the attic room. So, cautiously, he crept upstairs. The map lay on the floor and he could see that it was smeared with green slime. Reluctantly, Jake picked it up. Without any warning, a scream pierced the air...

See what I mean? Here are some ideas for writing gripping scenes:

1. 'Sentences of 3'
Use a 'sentence of 3' to build up the pace. For example:
...he hauled himself up the tree, crept carefully along a large branch and stopped opposite the window.

2. Powerful verbs

Use powerful verbs to add punch to your writing. Compare these two following sentences and you'll see what I mean:

Jake <u>got hold</u> of the rope and <u>climbed</u> up the tree.
<u>Gripping</u> tightly, Jake <u>hauled</u> himself up the old oak tree.

3. Short sentences

Dropping short sentences into your writing changes the pace of the story and can help keep your readers' interest.

But he missed!
It was too quiet.
Jake froze.

4. Adverb starters

Adverb starters can show how a character acts and feels.
For example:

> *<u>Reluctantly</u>, Jake picked up the map.*

5. Sentence openers

Try to vary the way you start sentences by using clauses to

emphasise the character's actions. For example:
Grasping the window ledge, Jake clung on.

6. An unexplained noise
Introduce an unexplained noise to really keep your readers gripped! For example:
At that moment he heard a scratching sound that seemed to be coming from downstairs...

WRITING TIP

Collect some suspense paragraph starters in your writing journal, such as:
suddenly···without warning···silently···in terror···in horror···a scream pierced the air···

---

7. The unexpected
Revealing just a glimpse of something unexpected can add heaps of suspense to your story. For example:
The map lay on the floor and he could see that it was smeared with green slime...

PACE YOURSELF
When you come to writing your mystery story, try and see what is happening in your mind. But remember you don't need to write down every detail. Too much

description can slow down the pace of your story. So keep the plot going by focusing on the key scenes. Miss out anything that isn't essential, like what your characters eat for breakfast or what they do when they are getting ready for bed, unless these scenes develop your plot or tell your reader something new about them.

On the other hand, don't rush the story to the point where you simply report what happened. For example, look at this dreadful ending: *The police arrived. Fingers McClary got caught. We all went home.* Try to vary your sentences and keep the pace moving. A better ending here would go something like this: *The police arrived in a flurry of blue flashing lights. They grabbed Fingers McClary, handcuffed him and pushed him into the back of the police car. Satisfied, we strolled home, wondering what our next investigation would be.*

FURTIVE FINALES AND NAIL-BITING ENDS!

Just before the ending you may want to build up the suspense by having a final dramatic event – the worst thing that has happened so far! This will keep your readers' guessing until the very end…

Jake dashed out of the alley. He was about to turn the corner when Crabbit grabbed him and dragged him through the gate of number 38. The gate swung shut. There was a silence while Jake struggled in vain. Crabbit clasped his hand over Jake's mouth to stop him calling out and a moment later he discovered why. The Stroud Hill Gang had followed him!

They pounded out of the alley and turned up the hill. As the sound of their feet faded, Crabbit released his hand. He could smell

Crabbit's breath as he whispered, 'Mr Sykes wants to speak with you, sonny, and he ain't too pleased.' Jake shuddered. He was alone now and no one knew where he was...

TYING UP THE LOOSE ENDS

Now that you have reached the end of the story it is important to tie up any loose ends in your tale. The reader is desperate to know what really happened, who did it and why! Think about some of these ways to tie up the threads of your story.

1. A gathering of suspects

In this type of ending a character, probably the sleuth, explains what has been happening to a gathering of people. The detective explains what really happened, revealing the clues they followed that led them to the culprit – who may be in that very room! When the villain is revealed you could have them confess everything! For example: *White-faced, Mr Jenkins stood up, coughed and lowered his head. 'I think I had better explain,' he stammered.*

2. Talking it through

Another way to end your mystery is when the events are revealed through two characters talking. This could be in person or over the telephone.

3. A letter or diary

Another interesting way of tying up the mystery is to have the ending revealed in a letter that explains the events, or even an extract from someone's diary. For example:

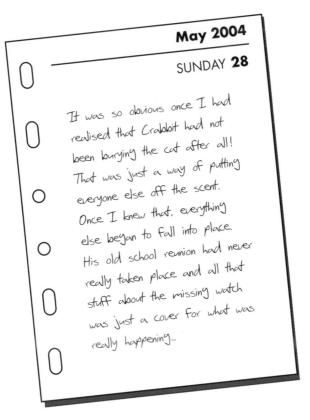

May 2004

SUNDAY **28**

It was so obvious once I had realised that Crabbit had not been burying the cat after all! That was just a way of putting everyone else off the scent. Once I knew that, everything else began to fall into place. His old school reunion had never really taken place and all that stuff about the missing watch was just a cover for what was really happening...

Make sure that by the final page of your mystery your readers know exactly what has happened. Nothing is worse than a dramatic build-up to a story, then not finding out who did it or why!

Here are some useful sentence starters to help you when tying up the threads of your tale:

At long last Trev knew why...
So, it had been Mr Potter after all who had...
They had been well and truly fooled by the old lady...
It was obvious now what had happened...
Finally, Polly could understand the reason why...

TIME TO WRITE

Now it's time to write your story!

Go back in your journal and refresh your mind about the plot. When you are writing, use the list of scenes to help shape each chapter. Remember the following things:

★ start your story with a bang to really capture your readers' attention;
★ establish the main 'sleuth' character early on;
★ build up the mystery problem at the start to really grip your readers!
★ describe the mystery in thrilling detail to make it exciting;
★ use red herrings to mislead the reader but also drop in clues about the mystery;
★ use suspense techniques to keep your readers on the edge of their seats;
★ use cliffhangers to really add drama;
★ tie up all the clues and reveal the mystery at the end.

EDITING AND PUBLISHING

POLISHING YOUR TALE

So you've finished your story – well done! What next?

Nearly all writers will tell you the same thing – you have to read it aloud! Have you missed anything out? Does the story flow? Does the tension build up? Can the writing be improved? Is it accurate?

EDITING YOUR STORY

It can help to put your story aside for a few weeks. When you get it out again, try to re-read it as though you have never seen it before. This will help you to spot the places where some rewriting might improve the story. Is your story gripping? Does it make you want to read on? Ask a friend to read it through for you and give you their opinion.

All stories that you buy from bookshops have been checked like this by an editor. An editor reads an author's work, suggests possible improvements and corrects any inaccuracies before it is published as a book.

Here are some things that you (or your friend) might look out for:

1. Possible improvements

☆ Does the beginning grip the reader?

☆ Is the mystery sufficiently interesting to make the reader want to read on?

☆ Is the main character likeable?

☆ Is the action exciting?

☆ Have you planted red herrings to lead the reader astray?

☆ Have you planted enough real clues but kept them well hidden so the reader is kept guessing until the end?

☆ Have you used suspense techniques to build tension?

☆ Have you made good use of cliffhangers?

☆ Is there a final crisis?

☆ At the end does the story tie up all the loose threads and explain the mystery in a satisfying manner?

2. Checking for accuracy

Make sure that your spelling, punctuation and
paragraphing are all correct.

Spelling checklist

If you cannot remember a spelling, you can:

☆ Say the word slowly, listen to each sound and write
   them down.

☆ Write the word down, look at it and adjust the spelling
   until the word looks right.

☆ Think of a word you can spell that rhymes with the
   word you want. The spelling might be similar.

☆ Work out if there are any suffixes, prefixes or a root
   word that you can spell.

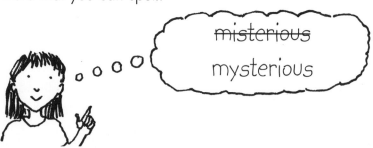

misterious
mysterious

☆ Break the word into syllables and tackle each part at a time.

☆ Use a dictionary or a computer spell check.

Don't avoid using a word because you cannot spell it. Try your best, and when you find out what the correct spelling is, make a note of it in your writing journal to remember for next time.

Punctuation checklist

☆ Make sure that each sentence makes sense and uses a verb (unless it is a one word sentence, such as 'OK?')

☆ Don't forget exclamation marks after exclamations, such as *Go on!*

☆ Remember to use question marks after questions, such as *Where did he go?*

☆ Don't forget commas to separate the things in a list, such as a list of clues – apart from the final 'and'. For example, *She picked up the packet, the old coin, the strip of paper and the map.*

☆ Use a comma to separate an adverb start, such as:

Go on!

Where did he go?

Carefully, she opened the envelope and peered inside.

☆ Use a comma to separate 'ing' and 'ed' starts, such as: *Wondering why the car had slowed down so much, Connor ducked down behind the hedge and waited.*

☆ Use a comma to separate a subordinate clause at the start of a sentence, such as: *While Crabbit explained about the cat, Connor noticed that the table was set for three people, not two.*

☆ Use a comma when you drop a phrase or clause into a sentence, such as: *Connor, slipping the envelope into his pocket, made his way towards the door.*

☆ Use speech marks to surround what is spoken (including any punctuation marks in the speech). Use a comma to lead into what is said. When a new speaker says something, start on a new line. For example:

'I'm sorry about the cat,' said Connor.

Crabbit replied, 'It never caught any mice anyway.'

Paragraph checklist

Long paragraphs can be hard to read. Don't put your readers off!

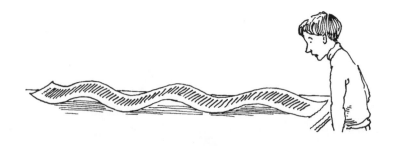

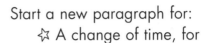

Start a new paragraph for:

☆ A change of time, for example:

Early the next morning...

☆ A change of place, for example:

On the other side of the mountain stood...

☆ A change of action, for example:

At that moment the lights went out...

☆ A change of character, for example:

Unexpectedly, Dr Townley rounded the corner...

PUBLISHING YOUR STORY

After all the time and effort you have put into writing your story, you now want some readers. You can publish your story in lots of different ways:

☆ read it aloud;

☆ email it to friends;

☆ turn it into a booklet to give to people;

☆ make a tape recording of it;

☆ post it on a website.

USEFUL ADDRESSES

☆ Young Writer

This is the national magazine for young writers – and it's brilliant! It has lots of ideas and tips about writing, in-depth interviews with well-known writers and competitions to enter. It also publishes young writers' stories and poems. You can visit the magazine's website at www.youngwriter.org or phone 01544 318901.

☆ www.stonesoup.com

This website belongs to another magazine for young writers. It provides links to loads of other great sites. These will put you in touch with other young writers, and give you top writing tips and opportunities to publish your writing on the web.

☆ Kids on the Net

This website invites children from age 6 to 16 to submit their writing for publishing on the web! Visit the website at www.kidsonthenet.com and why not send them one of your mystery stories?

☆ Creative Writing 4 Kids

This is a website where children can upload their work on to their own web pages. You could be just a mouse click away from becoming a published writer! Visit the website at www.creativewriting4kids.com.

WRITING TIP

Don't forget to give your story a really gripping title. Many writers leave this until the end as they find that a title often comes to them as they write. Most writers spend a while making lists of ideas. Mystery stories often have the word 'mystery' in the title. For example: The Mystery of the Spotted Snake or The Three Bells Mystery. Other words that you could use instead of 'mystery' are: riddle, puzzle, enigma, secret or problem.

Find the right title – and you're finished! Now make sure you publish the results of your hard work!

GLOSSARY

adjective A word that describes somebody or something, eg the <u>red</u> shoes.

adverb A word that adds meaning to a verb, eg *He ran <u>quickly</u>.*

alibi An alibi provides evidence that a person accused of a crime was somewhere else when it was committed.

alliteration A sound effect caused when a sound is repeated, eg *They <u>r</u>an <u>r</u>ound the <u>r</u>ugged <u>r</u>ocks.*

backstory Dropping in clues about a character's past life without being too obvious.

characterisation Revealing character through what they do, say, think, feel as well as description.

clause A group of words built around a verb, eg <u>She was angry</u> but <u>she didn't shout.</u>

cliffhanger An event that ends abruptly, leaving a character in a dangerous situation.

comma A punctuation mark (,) used to separate parts of a sentence or items in a list.

connective A word or phrase used to link ideas and events, eg *<u>Later on</u>, the dwarf fell asleep.*

dialogue The words that characters speak.

exclamation A sudden expression of emotion using an exclamation mark, eg *Help!*

metaphor The technique of writing about something as if it were something else, eg *The robber scampered away on mouse's paws.*

motive A character's reason for doing something.

mystery A story built around an unexplained event.

paragraph A group of sentences that make up a section of writing. New paragraphs begin at a change of time, place, speaker or focus.

personification A technique in which objects are given human characteristics, eg *The wind moaned.*

phrase A group of words that work as one unit, eg *the grey-haired, old lady.*

powerful verbs Verbs that show action and are expressive, eg *dashed, scuttled* or *darted,* to describe how a character moves.

prepositional phrase A group of words that explains where something is, eg *at the end of the road.*

red herring A false clue, used to keep the reader guessing.

'sentence of three' Links in a sentence, useful for description and pace, eg *He wore a hat, a coat and a pair of baggy trousers.*

settings Where a story takes place.

simile A technique in which the writer compares one thing to another, eg *The moon was as thin as a fingernail.*

simple sentence A sentence of one clause, *eg The man was scared.*

sleuth A character who tries to solve a mystery.

speech marks Punctuation marks ('') used to enclose spoken words.

speech verb A verb used to state how dialogue is spoken, eg *said, cried, muttered, yelled, explained.*

suspects Characters who might be responsible for villainy.

suspense Building up tension in a story.

timeshift A section in a story where action moves back or forwards in time.

villain The criminal responsible for a crime.

INDEX